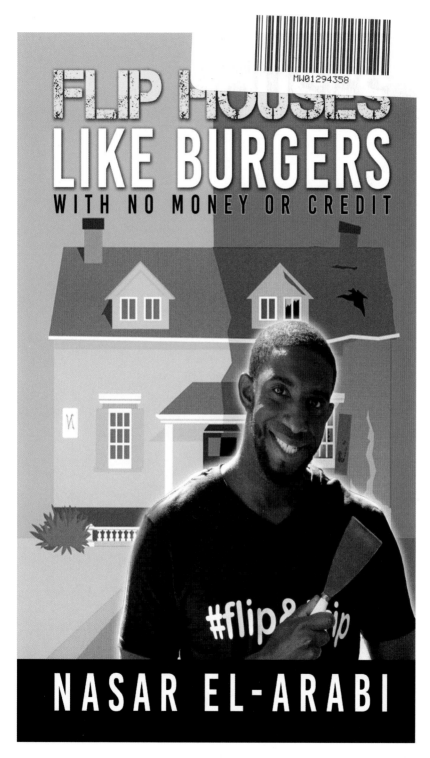

FLIP HOUSES
LIKE BURGERS
WITH NO MONEY OR CREDIT

#flip&flip

NASAR EL-ARABI

Table of Contents

Introduction

Allow me to introduce myself to you. My name is Nasar El-arabi. I currently live in Charlotte, NC and I am a six-figure real estate earner. I have had much success in a short period of time. Well, it does not feel like that, but that's what people at my local Real Estate Investment Association tell me. I am currently a rehabber, a wholesaler and a landlord.

However, it was not always like this, and before we jump into the meat and potatoes please allow me to give the back-story on myself. I promise not to bore you out. You bought this book to learn how to wholesale houses so I won't go too far into the fluff.

I had two loving parents, both from North Carolina, my mom from Lumberton and my father from Candor. They relocated to New Jersey back in the 70's for more opportunities. My sister and I were raised in Elizabeth, which is in northern NJ. We were probably 20-30 minutes outside of New York City, when there is no traffic to slow you down.

Growing up near New York gave me countless resources to start my entrepreneurial journey. Let me tell you about my first run-in with entrepreneurship. I was about eight years old and the school gave me candy bars to sell for a fund raiser. My mother was a school teacher for the Newark Board of Education and proud alumna of North Carolina Central University. My father was a car salesman. I was eight, so I just gave them the candy to sell to adult people.

We were middle class; however, being that we grew up in NJ a lot of times middle class was HOOD. It seems like in NJ you are rich or poor. There's really not a lot of in between. So my parents just wrote me a check for $40 to pay for the candy. I took the check to school and submitted it.

The candy though was still sitting in the house. I thought nothing of it at the time. Anyway, I was a big fan of the cartoon Darkwing Duck. And Darkwing Duck would run these commercials on TV advertising toys. Now, my parents were excellent providers; however, for whatever reason they did not think I needed more toys. Again, I was eight, so I needed as many toys as possible. A light bulb went off. I asked them if I could sell the candy that was in the house, save my money, and then buy my own Darkwing Duck toys. They agreed and an entrepreneur was born.

I would go everywhere with my parents and offer the candy at the doctor's office, and to parents, friends, and strangers. I was an adorable kid—at least, I like to think so. So people just bought the candy from me. My parents made me save the money. They opened me a bank account and all. I made 40 bucks and all the candy was sold.

Now that I actually worked for my money I did not want the Darkwing Duck toys any more. Its crazy, but when you earn something you don't want to release it as easily as if you did not work for it. I told my mother I just wanted to keep saving.

I came up with an idea to earn more money and presented it to my father. I had seen this thing on TV and thought it would be great for me to do. It was an "allowance." I asked my father for an allowance. And I think I started off at 5 bucks a week. I would do my chores and get paid. I was addicted to saving.

Years went by and now I was in middle school. I told my father I wanted to sell incense. He said okay and funded the business. For any of you who don't know, incense is these brown things that you burn to make the house smell good. I was 13 or so and I guess I was not that adorable any more, because no one bought from me. I was selling a pack for one American dollar and folks still turned me down. How can an adult say no to a kid selling anything for one dollar?

I will tell you what a mess it was trying to sell to a bunch of broke miserable adults. I did not know then but I understand now the people I was trying to sell to barely had their noses above water. One person even told me they can could get bigger incense and more for the same price I was selling mine for. C'mon, really? I was 13—you couldn't even give me a dollar for trying?

And there you have it. I quit that business as it did not work for me.

The next year something drastic happened. I lost my mother June 5th, 1996. It was shocking, to say the least. The night before she was happy and smiling. She came in, and I ran downstairs and told her I loved her. The next morning my father came in my room in a panic. I had never seen him like this before. We had to get dressed and there was a hospital driver outside. I sat in the back with my sister, who is three years older than me. We got to the hospital and the doctors told us my mom had died. I cried for weeks and still pray for her to this day. Anyway, she died in her sleep from heart disease. I was 14 years old.

When I tell people this story I always tell them they don't have to feel sorry for me. My mom died early in life but she taught me many valuable lessons I still heed today. My father and mother were married, and where I'm from that's a luxury, to say the least. They were married "till Death do us part", literally.

My father was a great provider. When I was a kid in the 90's he took us to see the greats. We saw Michael Jordan, Troy Aikman, Patrick Ewing, Shaquille O'Neal. If it was something I wanted to see or do, we did it.

I recall when I was a kid Wrestlemania was at Madison Square Garden in New York. My mom took me to the fan festival event. That was epic.

We traveled to NC every year, went to Disneyland as kids, and were always well dressed. So I really don't have bad memories of my parents. Thanks to this real estate business I was able to take my father to the 2014 Superbowl in NJ. Hopefully the things this business has been able to do for me, it will do for you as well.

Alright, now at this point I am in high school, and people, when I tell you I was Zack Morris of "HS", take my word. I was like Dwayne Wade from "A Different World". If you asked anybody where was the Nasar locker they would tell you down the hall on the right. I had business booming in my locker: white Tees, video games and jerseys.

I was quite the hustler in high school. I was also class clown, best dressed, and master of the art of being late to class. I literally did nothing in school but be cool. I played football and ran track, but coaches would not take me seriously because I was always joking.

Anyway, when it was time to apply for college not many colleges wanted to be associated with me. I graduated with a 1.8 average and probably had a 620 SAT score. And you get 400 points for spelling your name. I believe the highest score at that time was like a 1600. I got a 620.

I was heartbroken when my top school, Morgan State, turned me down. I had this smart girl write the entry essay and they still told me no. I tried my mom's *alma mater,* North Carolina Central University in Durham, NC. I just knew they were going to let me in, especially since I put my mom's name down as someone I knew who graduated from there. That did not work at all.

I got turned down from maybe 10 schools; most were out of state. University of North Carolina, Chapel Hill was my dream school, as well as Florida State. Even a stupid individual such as myself knew not to disrespect the Admission board with my foolishness. But I even got rejected from Berkeley College in NJ and if you don't know what Berkeley College is that's similar to getting rejected from playing for the Oakland Raiders. You know, you're sitting thinking, like, *really*? Y'all got better options?

Finally one college was dumb enough to accept me. The name of the college was Wilberforce University in Ohio. I had never been to Ohio and never heard of the college. It was a lady in Elizabeth, NJ who was getting people into the school. I mean anybody: literally, guys just coming home from juvenile detention, and all.

I said, well, it's college and girls will be there, so let's do it. I hopped on the Greyhound and met other people heading to Wilberforce University.

Freshman Orientation week had to be one of the best weeks of my life. We didn't do anything but have a bunch of FUN. Me being big man on campus, I found this girl willing to go back to my room to watch a movie on my Playstation 2, which was also a DVD player. We got to the desk and the security person said, "We can't have visitation rights yet." Wait one minute: I'd been watching "A Different World", "Saved by the Bell", "College Years" and other college-related television shows. And nobody ever said anything about waiting for visitation rights. Matter of fact, girls and guys are normally in the same dorm in those shows. But not at Wilberforce University: it was one boys' dorm, one girls' dorm and they had a Co-ed dorm just built.

In order to be in the co-ed dorm you had to be an Honor Roll student. So I knew right then and there I was going to miss that opportunity. Anyway, after a horrible four months I decided not to come back.

I transferred to another school, William Patterson University in NJ. All I did was eat and sleep. After the semester my GPA was 0.6. Yes, you read that correctly. I looked at my student loan balance and thought, I am taking out loans, however I am doing nothing in school. Maybe I need to step back and go to community college to see if school really is for me.

So that's what I did. I went to Essex County College and finished there in three years with my Associate's degree. Then I transferred to Kean University and finished in 2007. It took me six years to get my B.A., with a lot of cheating, a lot of nights buying essays from megaessay.com and this other site called chuckiii.com to get free essays. I was 24 and graduated in 2007. But I did it. Sometimes in life things start out bad but that doesn't mean they have to stay that way.

Let's talk about how I got into real estate when I was 19 years old. The guy next door sold to an investor and one day the investor showed up to the house with a brand new Range Rover and the this beautiful woman hopping out of the passenger seat. I was sold at that point. To put the icing on the cake I heard my father telling his friend the guy bought that house for $150K, put $20K into it, and sold it for $270K. I'm no mathematician but that added up to $100K profit in my head.

I went to my father and asked him how do I get into real estate. I mean, of course: if you want to get in to real estate the best person to ask is someone who does not do real estate. He told me his friend fixes your credit rating to prepare you to buy a house. I went to him to get my credit rating fixed and five years later, at 24, I was buying my first house. At the time I was still an undergrad and interning at MTV. I was a Communications major.

I did everything wrong in buying that first house. Eight months after the purchase we were able to sell, fortunately taking only a $7k loss each. We did everything wrong, literally. I won't get into details here because this whole book is focused on wholesaling. Basically, we watched "Flip that House" and all the other flipping shows and figured that we could do it. I mean all we had to do was buy a house, yell at some contractors and make a bunch of money. I knew I was going to get my check and buy a Bentley GT coupe while living at home with my father. But it did not work out like that.

After taking my defeat and eating my humble pie. I was ready to relocate to Charlotte, NC. I packed up and got ready to get out of NJ. I lined up my apartment and everything. Three days before leaving I called the apartment complex I was moving into...and found out they just got bought out and my application was not processed. I had been dealing with the rep for months, but of course the rep was no longer there. I already gave everything I had to the moving company.

Well, you know, when something can go wrong, it does. I said, I've got to get out of Jersey by any means necessary. I had goals to take over the real estate game in Charlotte. I was young, stupid and had a college degree. The world could not tell me anything. I moved down there and stayed in a hotel for like four days until I could get an apartment. Then I called the moving company with the new address.

Three months later, after a bunch of partying, I was able to get me a full-time gig at a call center. My first real job after college: I was making $10 an hour, going fast down Dead End Street.

I scheduled my days off during the week so I could interview for other jobs. I got another job after three months. There were people at that call center job for 10-plus years. I used to look at them and say to myself, "HELL NO, NOT ME". They kept me motivated and focused. I refused to have my future look like $11 an hour.

Anyway, after three months I got a job installing cable. I lasted all of three weeks. Climbing under houses and being handy is not for me.

I got a call from a major Fortune 500 company to work in their call center. I got the job and it was GOOD BYE, cable. I was at the headquarters at this job making like $12.50 an hour. It is a major bank that promised promotions and all that good stuff. I said to myself, I can sacrifice for a year and then move on to another department.

The method they used on me is called the corporate dream. Anyway, I was very arrogant: you could not tell me anything.

I bought a rental property in 2008 the traditional way, through a realtor. And I bought another one in 2009. I was young with properties. I should be running the company. And that's the attitude I went in there with. I soon learned that was a bad idea. Never discuss BIG GOALS with SMALL MINDED people. My co-workers liked me but the managers were not too fond of me.

One day I set up a meeting with the site director to talk to him about my career, because after I had served my year I felt things were not moving fast enough. I told him about my rentals, my goals, and the fact that $12.50 an hour was not working for me. I needed at least double. He recommended a book called Rich Dad, Poor Dad, by Robert Kiyosaki.

He never really spoke to me again after that meeting. The tension was real with me in that place. But that book changed my life and I understood that self development was something I needed to do.

I joined my local Real Estate Investment Association after that as well. I would have to use my vacation time to attend the main meetings. I didn't care: the thought of learning how not to work a job for 40 years kept me willing to do anything for my success.

After two years at this company and going back to college to work on my MBA on their dime. I realized I was not going to have a bright future with them. I left this company in 2010.

I started a new job with a very prestigious company in the financial sector. When I first started there I was reading another book by Kiyosaki called Retire Rich, Retire Young. This book helped me make the decision not to return to finish my MBA and to work at developing a real estate business.

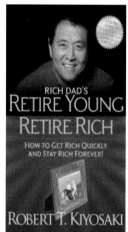

I was approached by a mentor who offered his services, I accepted, and eight months later I got my 1st wholesale deal, in 2011. I made $2000, and after paying my mentor took home $1300 or so. That was the start of something GREAT.

However, you can't live off of $1300. And at my job things were not going so well. They figured I was stupid. That was fine. I know I'm not that bright.

But, in November they called me into the office and of course I was late. I was in the bathroom taking a crap. I did not know that my manager had some crap for me.

They told me my position was being eliminated. They told me I didn't have to come in to work anymore, but they would pay me until January. And in January they would lay me off and my severance pay would start.

That was all right with me. I was playing around with the idea of doing real estate full time. I took my good friend Dan to lunch, and he gave me the advice to go back to work and make the perfect transition by leaving corporate America with enough cash flow to cover my living expenses. I felt as though he was right and went back to work. I was wholesaling houses meanwhile.

I got a new job in February at another major banking company. My job title was Policy Review

Analyst. I knew that title was going to get me some ladies. That stuff just sounds smart. But I kept messing up at the job. I could not do the work. I will admit I kept making errors. I was stressed out, and the stress was showing in my face. People that knew me were asking what was going on.

But before I got fired, I got two job offers that I turned down. My friend Wyndia back in Jersey told me, "Nasar, you can always get another job, but you will be 29 only once." That was all the confirmation I needed.

Then, in September, my grandpa died, I told my job I needed some time off to attend his funeral. I guess they said, "This is a great opportunity to tell him not to come back." So that's what happened: they fired me. I'm still pissed they made me work the whole day when they were letting me go. They easily could have fired me before rush hour.

It was time to show up now. When you are in any start-up business there is no time to be sitting around twiddling your thumbs. That's how you end up back at a job for someone else within three months. Fortunately, my 9-5 was funding my 5-9. So when my 5-9 became my 9-5, it was not an extremely hard transition.

Besides, I learned from some really smart people: Jay Parker, Dan Gosser, Laurie Knisely and Sean Terry. The first three names you probably never heard of because they are local investors who are super smart and successful, not national figures. I attended their meetings and worked with them as if my life depended on it.

Any way, that's my story. Now I want to get into actually HOW to wholesale houses. Since I was fired I've been able to travel, take my father to the Super Bowl, buy a house for my primary residence, paint my dad's house and create a six-figure business by wholesaling houses. I went from being worth $38K a year, which was my salary at the last job I got fired from, to now sometimes making that in a month.

Now it's your turn to change your life. Let's hop into how to wholesale houses.

What is Wholesaling Houses?

Wholesaling houses is basically where a person finds houses at a deep discount, contracts the property and sells the interest he has in the property to an end user, also known as a cash buyer or investor.

Do you need a Real Estate license to wholesale real estate? No you do not. Real Estate Agents sell houses for people. As investors we can sell houses we own; in this case we will be selling paper. We exercise our contract rights to assign properties to someone else. We are not representing home owners or buyers. That job is for Real Estate Agents. We are contracting great deals and simply assigning our Contracts to an end user.

Let's do a Case Study

I recently found a house. We'll say it's at 123 Main St, Charlotte, NC 12345. I found it through direct mail (we will discuss more about finding houses later).

The seller gave me the address to the property. While I was on the phone with the seller, I went to www.zillow.com, put the address in and looked at sold houses only in the area. Houses with a similar size in square feet, with about the same number of bedrooms and baths, were selling around $190K. The seller wanted $80K and we settled on $79K. The house needed a complete renovation. I met with the seller and we signed a contract. The seller gave me the contract and I called a buyer who likes the area and sold it to him for $97K. This left me with an $18,000 spread to pick up at the closing.

Disclaimer: Results may VARY! Every deal will not be a HOME RUN!

Now, the process is simple but not easy. So let's address some questions:

Why will a seller take such a low offer on his property?
I don't know why people do what they do. I look at people who smoke, drink and party and I'm lost about why they would do such things with their lives. However, a few reasons might be because they do not want to deal with realtors and looking for a quick cash offer from an investor. The houses we deal with in most cases WILL NOT GET APPROVED FOR A LOAN. I have had sellers contacting me after they contacted a realtor who wanted them to put thousands of dollar they don't have into a property before the agent would take the listing. Most people in the country live pay check to pay check and don't have $15K to bring their house up to current market conditions.

They are in distress and need someone to come to them and walk them through the process (you are the professional so they are trusting: you remember that).

These are just a few reasons a seller might take a lower offer. Please don't get caught up in the analytics. We are here to assist these people with our services in their time of need. WE

DO NOT TAKE ADVANTAGE OF PEOPLE. If you think this is a way to take advantage of people, please do not do this business as you will only give all of us a bad name.

Why can't cash buyers find their own houses?

A lot of time cash buyers don't have time to do all the marketing and effort that goes into finding great deals. So they'd rather just pay people like us to find great deals. I myself buy deals from wholesalers and I market to sellers my self. The reason why is that I can't and won't get every great deal on my own. A seller sells when they are ready. That means that I might send them a letter in February and get nothing, but when you send them a letter in July they call you because your timing was perfect. It's part of the business: it happens.

I would never sell my house for a low price. I would want full price Nobody can possibly be this stupid.

First off, these people are not stupid: they are in need of help because traditional ways won't work for them. Second, YOU ARE NOT YOUR CLIENT. I personally would never sleep outside to be first in line for a video game, sneakers or a Black Friday sale. But guess what? People do it all the time. And companies make billions from offering their products to them.

Step by Step

Moving along, let me try to break the process down step by step, in case some folks did not get the previous example.

1. You find a motivated seller.
2. You guys agree on a fair price, let's say $46K.
3. You sign a contract.
4. You tell your buyers about the property.
5. You show buyers the property at $59K. A buyer makes an offer at $56K. You assign your contract to the buyer.
6. Everything goes to an attorney or title company for processing.
7. The deal closes and you pick up a check for $10K.

It's really that simple, even if it is not easy. Please try not to over-complicate things. I will break down each step in detail to help you better understand. After all, that's why you got this Ebook.

Step 1. Find Motivated Sellers

There are many ways to find motivated sellers. My two main ways are **direct mail** and **bandit signs**. I do have a website that gives me leads as well.

A website is not a make or break thing for you. A website is like having a business card. It makes you feel good, and impresses some folks. Once you have it you need to work it via SEO or Adwords campaigns. Please be careful with using Adwords, though, as you can get hurt financially if you don't know what you are doing. I know guys who lost as much as $7K on a single Adwords campaign.

For finding motivated sellers my favorite strategy is **direct mail**. You have to buy a list from a list broker like www.listsource.com, www.flipthisrealestatelist.com, or just Google "list brokers". In some cities you can get list from your city.

ListSource™   BUILD LIST   QUICK LIST

Build Your Local or National Marketing Lead List with Fresh and Precise Property and Homeowner Information

When I buy a list I go after absentee owners with at least 10 years of equity. So if they took a mortgage out it was more than 10 years ago. I like to mail them. Also you must have zip codes you want to target. If you go to flipthisrealestatelist.com, ask for his Vacant house list. It costs a little more but is well worth it.

FLIP THIS REAL ESTATE LIST
"ANY REAL ESTATE LIST YOU NEED LOWEST PRICE GUARANTEED"

Once you purchase a list go to **yellowletters.com** and pick out a post card or a yellow letter to mail from their site. They do everything for you. If you have your own post card you can upload it to **Click2mail.com**. If you have trouble using any site, calm down and just contact their customer service. They will be more than happy to help you.

Let's say you are broke like I was when I first started. It took me eight months to find my deal after getting a mentor. I was **driving for dollars**, aka farming neighborhoods, aka cruising for cash. I would look for houses with tall grass, beat up roofs, and boarded up windows—ugly houses and houses that were vacant with a for rent sign. I would write these addresses down in my notebook. I did this every Saturday—you must be dedicated for this to work. I've seen some people get deals the first time they try, but it's really not typical.

On Sunday I would cross-reference the address on my city assessment site. That means I would type the address into my city assessor's site to get the owner of the property. If there was a good address I would write them a post card. I used to buy post cards from the local post office or usps.com.

I would write out a simple message:

> I would like to buy your house at 124 Main st.
> Please call 123 456 7899
> Sincerely,
> Nasar

It was very effective. At this time of me writing this in 2015, a pre-stamped post card is 38 cents. So 100 will be $38.00. I would buy packs of 100 through their website. In person for some reason they usually don't have a lot in stock. This has been my personal experience.

When I drove for dollars I would stay out there for 2-4 hours. I would come back with three pages worth of addresses. I would then filter the list following my criteria, which is houses with no mortgage or bought 10 years prior to today's date. I use a system called **crsdata.net** that gives me mortgage information. It's not available in all areas. I was advised Realquest.com does the same thing. After eliminating the houses that did not meet my criteria I would mail out probably 20-30 post cards a week.

As far as having a number for your sellers to call I would recommend getting a **Google voice number**. It's FREE with each Gmail address. Be sure to turn off the features in options that make the person calling you state their name first. You do not want to annoy your clients. I use it and it's a very good tool to have.

You can also put this number on your **bandit signs**. Do not put your real numbers on the signs. It would be easy for the city to find you and fine you. Please check to see if bandit signs are permitted in your city. If they are not permitted please be aware you can face BIG FINES. Use the signs at your own risk. This ebook is not telling you to do things that will get you in trouble.

I like to get my signs from **www.dirtcheapsigns.com**. If you buy the signs from there, get the hand written font yellow sign and red letters. If you can't afford to order pre-printed signs, get blank signs and write them out.

Step 2. Agree to the Price

When I first started I would carry around a cue card with questions to ask the seller. The questions were:

> What is your name?
> What's the property address?
> May I ask you a few questions about the property?
> How many bedrooms?
> How many bathrooms?
> Is the house currently vacant or occupied?
> What is your situation? Why are you selling?
> What kind of repairs need to be done to the property?
> Do you have a mortgage?
> How much do you owe?
> We pay all cash and close quickly! How much are looking to get for this property?
> Is that the best you can do?

It's only right that I keep it real with you guys. Not every call will go smoothly, not every seller will cooperate with the flow, some sellers will asked to be removed from your list, and some sellers will curse you out. The worst I got was a seller who told me to get back on my camel and go back to my country. As far back as my GREAT grand parents, we are all American. Maybe someone needs to give that seller a lesson on the slave trade.

And I don't even have a camel. At one point the gas prices were so high I would have been honored to have a camel. Anyway, the moral of the story is that you must have tough skin. Entrepreneurship is hard. Okay, I said it for the 90th time. This will not be a walk in the park.

Now let's rewind a little bit to when you are on the phone with the seller and the call is going smoothly. Ideally you want to be in a location where you have your laptop open and you're on Zillow, redfin or any other comparison site. Please be mindful you are looking for closed sales only, not for a list that includes pending sales.

Go to my YouTube channel www.youtube.com/realestatedoru and search for the video titled HOW TO GET FREE REAL ESTATE COMPS. That video will show you me doing it on Zillow so you can follow along.

HOW TO GET FREE REAL ESTATE COMPS

Realestate Doru

▶ Subscribe 2,341

Let's say you see solds at $95-129K. That should be an indication that it's probably a homeowner area, being that sales are moderate. And this may vary per market. The seller knows their house is beat up. So they ask for $50K. You guys do some back and forth and settle on $45K.

Step 3. Sign the Contract

(go to realestatedoru.com to get free contract templates.)

With my offers I usually make a soft offer on the phone since I am a wholesaler. I have to get a lot of marketing out and if I were to go see every house, I would never be able to get things done.

To prevent running myself wild I do a soft offer over the phone, so while I am looking at comps I will say, "For this house I will be between forty and fifty thousand. Ideally I want to be at 45 thousand." After I say that I SHUT UP and listen. If they respond with an okay, that's fine. If it's dead silence and they don't say anything, after a bit I say, "So when can we set up an appointment?" That will get them to respond. If they say, "Absolutely NOT," I know right now they are not motivated. And I will follow up with them in a month or two. If they respond with any date or time, that is fine.

We set the appointment. I go out to take pictures of the property. These days you can take pics with your camera phone. I'll make my offer after viewing the property.

The way I do it is to come up with the average price similar homes in the area sold for (the AVR), and then apply my formula:

The Real Estate Doru OFFER Formula

(I like to say I am a "Doru", not a Guru, because I don't just know about stuff: I **do** it.)

ARV x .70 – Repairs – Your Profit = OFFER

Example

$117,000 x .70 = $81,900 - $25,000(repairs) – $10,000 (your profit) = $46,900(offer)

Potential gross profit if sold at full price to cash buyer: **$10,000**

Calculating repair costs

I know what some of you are thinking: "I do not know how to calculate repairs on a place". Great: I am full time and I'm not good at it either. So do not let that stop you from making offers. A great way getting started is bring someone experienced with you, get a contractor to get an estimate in exchange for you giving him some business in the future, or use the examples provided below to come up with a repair number.

Example estimates

Exterior

Roof: 0 - $8,000, depending on further inspection. You can get a price per square foot from several roofing contractors and use the average of their estimates. Considerations: if the plywood under the shingles is good and there is only a single layer of shingles, you can just add another layer. If there are already two layers of shingles, you have to remove the existing shingles before adding the new layer, and this is of course more expensive. And if the plywood is broken or damaged, you may have to rip everything off down to the bare joists— and even then you may find some rot or other problems. This is a lot more expensive.

Gutters: If the home needs new gutters, it will probably run to $1,000.

Chimney: 0-$15,000. As with roofing, you can get a price per square foot estimate from several contractors to come up with the market price for your area. Repointing some bricks or making the stucco coating look good will cost less than $1,000. At the other extreme is a chimney so damaged that you have to take it down and rebuild it. That's the high-high end of the estimate.

Masonry: 0-$3,000. For most homes, you just need to patch small areas on the sidewalks, steps and driveway. But you can't get a certificate of occupancy in many areas without fixing broken masonry. This estimate goes way up if something serious has happened, like a retaining wall starting to let go.

Landscaping: $500-a fortune. Just cleaning up the yard so it looks like someone cares about the property will eat $500. New plantings, young trees, rock gardens, retaining walls—they all cost a significant amount and really don't gain you very much unless you know the buyer wants exactly what you are planning to add.

Painting and trim work: $2,500-$6,000. If the property has been neglected for a while the high end may go even higher, because you may need to scrape and paint the exterior walls and touch up or completely repaint every interior space.

Exterior doors: Unless you are lucky, every new exterior door will run $500-$1,000 for purchase and installation.

Odds and ends: $500. You may need a new doorbell or a pretty welcome mat, and a lawn ornament.

Interior

Walls: $800-$4,000. The low end covers patching, sanding and touching up walls after normal wear and tear. If you have to replace sheet rock or framing, the price goes up.

Windows: $2,500-$4,000. Count on at least $200 per window; the cost may be higher for older homes because of non-standard window sizes.

Doors and trim: $1,000. Updating old interior doors will cost about $75 per door. Trim around the doors can be tricky to match and expensive.

Heating system: 0 - $4,000. If the heating system is old, replace it rather than trying to tinker with it. It will add dramatically to the resale value of the house.

Air conditioning: 0-$4,000. If the house has central air conditioning that is working, leave it alone. If the structure allows for adding one without too much effort, do it. The gain in resale value is significant.

Bathrooms: $1,000-$7,000. Allow $500 per bathroom just for minor renewal, such as a new toilet and medicine cabinet. Allow at least $2,500 for a thorough upgrade of each bathroom.

Kitchen: $3,000-$6,000, for standard counters and appliances.

Plumbing: $500-$10,000. Replacing all the sinks and taps will use up the first $500. The rest is for the nasty problems of older houses that you may run into.

Electrical: $500-$5,000. Replace all the switches and outlets and any un-cool built-in lighting features. If you need to replace the electrical panel, allow for about $2,000. New wiring will add that much again.

Floors: $2,500-$5,500. Get per-square-foot estimates for carpeting, snap floors, refinishing hardwood floors and linoleum from local contractors, to get a sense of costs in your area.

Fittings: $300-$500 to replace door hinges, door handles, and possibly window locks and similar hardware. The visual effect is very high for the cost.

Step 3a. Sign the Contract, continued

While viewing the property be sure to take lots of pictures of the house. Don't worry at first how they will come out. You get better at taking photos with time and practice. Take pictures of all rooms, front of house, back of house, hvac unit, roof, back yard—basically everything.

Now, you offered $40k but you guys went back and forth and agreed at $46k. I recommend you do negotiations in person and get the contract signed on the spot. However, I don't always do this. Sometimes I go back home, run the numbers and do some more negotiation over the phone. Most of my sellers are not in the 21st century so they do not have email. There have been been times I had to mail contracts with pre-paid envelopes to get them signed if the seller is out of state. Or you can email or fax the contract, use signing tools like dotloop.com or hellosign.com. Dotloop.com and Hellosign are not 100% FREE.. So if you are just now starting out don't worry about those. Hellosign however lets you sign three free contracts a month.

Let's say you guys are ready to sign the contract. I explain to the seller that I must get my money partners and contractors in the house to approve the deal. Your money partners are your people with the cash, of course. In most cases the seller has no issue with that. I put a lock box on the house with a key in it.

Step 4. Inform Your Buyers

I have a buyers list that's pretty strong and full of real buyers. So I just give them the lock box code to let themselves in. However, being that you are new, please limit your list while you are just starting out. A lot of people will tell you to find buyers first. I disagree, because as long as you can find motivated sellers you will stay in business. Having a bunch of buyers that you do not know if they will really bite once you bring the deal is not much of a money-maker. Buyers could be a money-maker once you get a strong list. I keep my buyers in a contact list I made in Gmail.

Real Estate Doru Method for Finding Buyers

1. Google "we buy houses"
   Call the number on any site in the search results that covers your area. Ask them are they buyers or wholesalers. If they say buyer take their information down and ask them what are they looking for. You can run your deal past them as well. If they say wholesaler ask them if they have a buyer for your deal or can you work together for future deals. You guys can split the assignment fee. If they are resistant, they are probably new and don't know what they are doing. I move on when people can't answer simple questions.

2. Real estate auctions
   This is a sure-fire way to get real buyers who are not tire kickers. Buying at the auction is an advanced strategy, however, and these buyers might not know what a wholesaler is. So please explain your wholesaling service to them and ask for a business card or contact information so you can shoot deals over to them for consideration.

3. Your Local REIA meeting
   You can find your local REIA meeting at nationalreia.com, or go to meetup.com type in your zip code and search the topic "real estate". Introduce yourself  and tell people what you do. Getting value out of this group might take a little bit of work because in most of these meetings the majority are not doing anything. You have to find the deal makers. Once you build a relationship with one action-taker he can point you in the direction of more.

4. Craig's List
   In full disclosure I do not use this to find buyers. In my city craigslist.com is full of tire kickers. However, results may vary per location. What you could do is put up an ad of your house in the Craigslist real estate owned section.

5. Call the number on a "we buy houses" sign
   In my city the majority of the "we buy houses signs" are wholesalers. However, that is fine. Ask them if they are a wholesaler or buyer. If they are a wholesaler tell them you have a deal and would they be interested in presenting it their buyers and you and they can split the assignment fee. If they are a buyer, put them on your list, ask them what are they looking for, and tell them about your current deal.

6. Pull cash transactions
   There are two ways to pull cash transactions. You can make friends with a realtor at your local REIA. You can offer them your leads you can't do anything with so they can potentially list them, give them short sales leads, and in a nutshell offer them some kind of value. Don't be a taker: be a giver. Believe me, if they think you are just another taker they will be quick not to pick up your calls. We are to be extra nice to them because they have FREE access to cash transactions in your area. However, not all realtors know they have access, so you might want to deal with investor-friendly realtors. Another way is to buy the list from a list broker like listsource.com or flipthisrealestatelist.com. Once you get the list, focus on the same zip code as your deal. Make a flyer, using Word or any text editor, of your deal. Mail the flyer to buyers.

Step 5. Show the Buyers the Deal

So now you are marketing the property's contract to your buyers list. As a new person its always good to meet buyers at a property and walk them through it. If you work during times when your buyer wants to see properties, its always good to work with a full-time wholesaler.

So let's say the buyer walks through the property and offers you $56k. You verbally agree to accept that. You tell him you need an $XXX earnest money deposit. On my properties that are $25k or lower and I know the buyer I will tell them $500 is sufficient. Now you will hear different things about collecting earnest money. I personally have the buyer write a non refundable deposit to the attorney / title company only. My state of NC is an attorney state so we close our deals with attorneys. You must check with your state law to see if you guys are in an attorney state or if you can use a title company to close your real estate deals.

Back to the money: I will have them write me a check to my attorney and we will sign the assignment. Also the buyer will need to see your original contract to see exactly what they are being assigned. So don't panic if they ask for the contract. I normally give a 10 day close. The reason I like buyers to write a check to the attorney is that I've seen wholesalers get deposits, spend the money and then the title comes back with some issues. The deal can't close and now that wholesaler is on the hook for that money.

You will have some buyers who will see what you're making and have a fit about it. I use one simple technique with them. I don't deal with them and REMOVE THEM FROM MY LIST. Never let your buyer control what you make. There are some exceptions to this rule: if he mentored you, walked you through the transaction, or you just don't mind cutting them a break because they helped you along the way. That's cool, but if a buyer agrees to buy the property at a set price verbally and then they see the contract and assignment and suddenly the numbers no longer work for them, I don't deal with them anymore. People will try to do to you what they won't want done to them.

One way to avoid a buyer seeing your assignment is to do a double closing (described later on). People say if you are making over $10k to do a double closing. I do the majority of assignments to me personally. If people bark at what I am making, then great: we wont do business.

Step 6. Send Everything to the Attorney or Title Company*

So the assignment of contract is signed, you've got the earnest money deposit and now you drop everything off at the attorney's or title company depending on your state. Now you will hear different opinions about this. Some people, once they get the contract they start the title search to ensure the title is good. I personally start the title search when I get a buyer.

Worst case scenario: if the title has issues the buyer gets his deposit back. In order for the buyer to get his deposit back, the seller must agree and sign something stating it's okay to give the seller back the deposit. The reason I wait to run the title is that I will be on the hook for the title search which usually runs $125-175 in my local area depending on the attorney. However, once you start closing deals consistently, attorneys will either charge you a reduced rate when deals don't close or waive the fee.

Another reason I start title search after I find a buyer is because some buyers will not use my attorney. If you are adamant about a buyer using your attorney/ title company, be sure to advise them of that up front. If they have to use their own attorney to close the deal get their attorney's information and call the attorney ask them do they do assignments. Also ask if they do double closings. If they do not do assignments tell your buyer you can't use that attorney. If he still insists on that attorney you must find a new buyer.

If they do **double closings** you still might be able to use an attorney who will not do assignments. With a double closing you have a contract with seller. Then you create another contract between you and the buyer. You will have to pay closing cost for a double close, since there are two contracts. The deed to the property is going from Seller A to buyer B (you), then from you (now the Seller) to your end buyer. Not only are there closing costs involved. Some attorneys might recommend you getting title insurance to protect yourself from any claims in the future. Typically closing costs run $300-500 and title insurance can be $150.00-500.00. Those numbers are not set in stone and could be different in your area.

Now for all the technical people, let me give you the proper definition of a title search. In real estate business and law, according to Wikipedia, a **title search** or **property title search** is the process of retrieving documents evidencing events in the history of a piece of real property, to determine relevant interests in and regulations concerning that property.

NEVER MENTALLY SPEND YOUR MONEY BEFORE CLOSING THE DEAL. We do not get paid until the deal is closed. Many things can go wrong between now and closing. The good news: I will say in my opinion 80% of title issues can be resolved. However, you have certain liens & judgments that can not be easily resolved. I had a deal for $70k and had a buyer lined up at $95k. The title came back and it had a IRS lien of $150k. The IRS would allow the sale to happen, however they were going to take 100% of sellers proceeds. As you can imagine, the seller suddenly was not in a rush to sell any more. IT HAPPENS. MOVE ON DON'T GET CAUGHT UP IN IT.

My personal opinion is that I think wholesaling is better as a volume based business and not depending on one deal to close. I do volume and always have stuff in the pipeline I am working on.

So let's say everything goes right with the title search. Then you have clearance to close and our favorite part will be coming up.

Step 7. The Deal Closes!

This is my favorite part! And if we are getting an assignment fee, we don't even have to show up. It might be a good experience to show up to your first two or three closings to see how simple a cash closing is. They literally take less than 15 minutes.

I typically do not show up to closings that are assignments for me. The only thing I show up for is to pick up my check. It feels good picking up those checks. To be honest, if you don't like to waste gas you can tell the attorney to wire the money to your bank account. In most cases you are charged a wire fee, typically no more than $25. However that option is totally up to you.

Now some of you are thinking what if seller gets to closing and sees another guy there signing documents. Will they be upset? Look, we are dealing with motivated sellers. They WANT TO SELL THEIR HOUSE. Also to protect myself, I tell the sellers up front, "At closing you will be closing with my money partners." Sellers normally want one thing out of the houses and that's relief from dealing with the issues related to their houses, and freedom to do whatever they are doing next.

I get asked if wholesaling is legal. Yes: we are assigning contracts. Unless they change contract law it will always be legal.

Let's step back here: you signed a contract with the seller for $46k and you assigned your contract to the buyer for $56k. At closing the buyer wires in $56k. The balance of $10k goes to you. It will show up on the HUD as an assignment fee. Some people like to get paid outside of the closing to avoid showing up on the HUD in fear of a seller getting upset. I did that on my first deal. My advice to you is to please make sure you trust to buyer to pay you. After people get what they want from you they might not be as nice to you. I always prefer to be on the HUD.

Then you will rinse and repeat this multiple times a year to get the desired results. Please be mindful that assignment fees may vary. It's no set price, as long as your buyer is getting a great deal. That's the most important thing here.

I hope the above breakdown was helpful. The most important thing is not to over-complicate the process.

Finding Motivated Sellers

The next thing we will cover in detail is finding motivated sellers. As long as you have sellers needing to sell their house you will always be in business.

Notice how I used the word NEED. We are not looking for people who just *want* to sell. We are looking for people who *need* to sell. It's a big difference between want and need. I want to have a 2017 Tesla. I need a roof over my head. You see where I'm going? I am looking for sellers who have headaches because I walk around with Advil in my pockets. (I got that from my mentor, Jay.)

The most successful people in the world are problem solvers. Steve Jobs saw a problem with people carrying around 5 CD's to be entertained on their daily commute, so he came up with the iPod. Malcolm X saw a problem with African Americans getting treated unfairly, so he started a revolution he will always be remembered by to get African American basic human rights. Harriet Tubman saw a problem with slavery so she freed slaves through the underground railroad. Henry Ford saw a problem with the way people were commuting, so invented the car.

Let's take out the money for a few minutes. Money does not make you successful. your impact on the world that makes you successful. And let me tell you, when you relieve these sellers they will be more than grateful.

Allow me to be honest with you for a second: if you want to be successful at this business, you need to realize that you are in the Sales, Negotiating and MARKETING. I strongly recommend you pick up books on sales. You are selling your service. You give relief to home owners. Also, it's good to get great at negotiating. As far as marketing, this will keep your bank account growing. Remember that the key to marketing is to get a response. I provide some ways to find motivated sellers. Once you get them on the phone, it's up to you to negotiate and close them.

Not everyone is motivated. Sometimes I send out a thousand post cards out and get NO DEALS. However, I follow up with the ones with a little motivation months later to see if they are ready for my price at that time.

Marketing to Motivated Sellers

Direct Mail Marketing is what it sounds like: it's mail delivered to people in hopes of getting some business. With direct mail marketing you can target or take the shotgun approach and mail everyone. I know people who used the mail-every-door option that the United States Post Office offers. However, they said they failed horribly. Marketing for a small business owner like ourselves, in my opinion, always works better when it's highly targeted.

The most popular mail piece that you probably heard of is the **Yellow letter**. The yellow letter is a hand-written letter, on a yellow sheet of paper, in a hand-written envelope. This can be great to get started on if you are on a budget. You can see many examples of this on yellowletters.com

You can also send out **post cards**, which are very inexpensive compared to letters. I first out with a hand-written stamped post card. I got pre-stamped post cards from usps.com. Back in 2011 I used to get 100 of them for $29.00. The price of course has gone up since then. Please check usps.com for pricing. I would write a simple message on the card. These were very effective. Pre-printed post cards are very good as well. The more you are able to send out, the better chance you have of getting a deal. For post card examples please go to yellowletters.com. You can call yellow letters or chat with them and ask for their most effective post cards.

Another method that is a great way to get leads are **bandit signs**. These are those "we buy houses" signs. Handwritten font or signs are way more effective then the professional pre-printed ones, I think because people are anti-corporation. They feel that big corporations will try to steal my house. However that Nasar guy from around the corner, we can get over on him. For this reason I strongly recommend you use a local FREE GOOGLE voice number on the sign.

Please check with your local municipality to see if bandit signs are legal. If they are illegal where you are located, please know I no longer endorse this stream of marketing for you.

I like to do 50 signs every other week. The first week I get 5-7 calls. However 100 signs a month gets me one deal. So you get less calls then mail, however people are a lot more motivated.

A **website** is like a business card: it's only effective if you work it. If a business card stays in your pocket it will not gain you business at all. If a website is not worked properly it will not be very helpful. Please allow me to say YOU DON'T NEED A WEBSITE. I've done many deals without a website. I know six- and a few seven-figure earners who don't have a website or business cards. I am simply going over a few marketing techniques.

One way to market a website is called **SEO**. SEO is Search Engine Optimization, a strategy to have your site appear near the top of search results for certain terms in Google or any search engine. We will use Google as an example. When you look at your search results in Google, you see paid ads along the right side, with two or three more ads above the results.

Your goal with SEO is to rank on the first page of search results without having to pay for ad space. That way when a seller searches "sell my house fast" you want to show up on that first page.

Another way to get traffic to a website is by paying for ads. The most popular ad system is **Google AdWords**. Please be extremely careful using this marketing strategy. I met people who have spent $7k in one campaign, with very little

to show for it. There will be a learning curve about how to run ads. And when I say learning curve I mean you will lose money. I know a guy who does six figures every six months with this tool, so it can be very worthwhile. You have to figure out do you want to out source this or learn how to do yourself.

Craigslist.com is another tool that can be used. Again you guys know I am the DORU and not a GURU. I will say this has not been effective for me. It does work for other people, though. In my city, Craigslist is full of fakers and wholesalers who don't know what they are doing. However, you can place your "we buy houses" ads on Craigslist for free. I have done a deal by doing this before, but don't hold your breath while doing it.

At this point I hope you are getting the picture of marketing. It's very important. Here are a few more ways you can market your service for people who NEED to sell their house.

- Newspaper ads
- Door hangers
- Signs on your car
- Billboards
- Radio ads

Generating Seller Leads

To stay in business you must always have leads coming, both old or new leads. We went over marketing, and now we must go over getting the leads.

One way to get leads is to go to Listsource.com. They are a list broker and there are many list brokers out there that can assist you. When using listsource.com you must know what criteria to put in. Please follow the steps below.

Creating an absentee seller list on listsource

1. Click "Build list".
2. Choose your country, city, or zip code.
3. Go to Property. For last market sale date select as a start 01/01/1900 and as an end date a date ten years from the current date.
4. For property type select residential single family, residential multi, residential duplex, residential triplex, residential quad, and townhouse. If you want, also select residential condominium and vacant land.
5. Under options select absentee owners (in and out of state).

That will give you a list you can get started on.

Another site you can visit is FlipthisRealestatelist.com. If you call or email this site tell him that Nasar said he can beat any other list broker's price. He will give you a special rate. He also sells probate leads, tax delinquent leads, code enforcement leads, vacant house leads, and so on. You must tell him your county to see if he offers his specialty list in your area. The specialty list costs a little more than your absentee owner leads; however the chances of motivation increase. If you can spend the money, I strongly recommend you get the vacant house leads.

Let's say you are starting out the way I did, FLAT BROKE. If you are looking for the "cheap as possible" plan you have to work harder than your competition. However, there is still hope for you. The strategy you can use is **driving for dollars** aka cruising for cash. This is where you will hop in your car, pick a neighborhood and drive around to look for beat up houses, not well kept houses, houses that need roof work, lawns with tall grass, boarded up homes, ugly houses, bbandoned houses and houses torn up from the floor on up. Please do not use your logic in this and say to yourself who will buy these ugly houses? Someone will buy anything if the PRICE IS RIGHT.

When I used to drive for dollars I would get about three notebook pages full of addresses from each little trip. Then I would go on my city assessment site. This site here might help you find your city assessment site: http://netronline.com/. Then you cross reference the addresses on your list with the entries on the site to see who owns each property. If the bank owns it I cross it off my list. If it was NOT brought at least 10 years prior from today's date I cross it off, unless I see they got a great deal or it has no mortgage. Chances are you will not be able to tell if the house has any mortgages on it. I use a paid-for system that gives me that information.

After eliminating the bad stuff you will probably have a small number of prospects to mail to. That's perfectly normal. At this point just write out a letter or hand written post card.

Another FREE way for generating leads is to farm for-sale-by-owner sites, Craigslist "for rent" ads and Craigslist "for sale" ads. With the for-rent ads you will tell them you are an investor in the area and would like to buy their house. Are they open to selling? Then you will start the conversation from there. Chances are pretty high that you will get deals the first ten times you do this. This is something you have to work consistently not just one time, though. That's true for the other strategies as well, because there is no short cut to success.

craigslist

post to classifieds

my account

As we already discussed, bandit signs will get you some motivated sellers on the line. If you are on a tight budget you can buy 18 by 24 blank signs and hand write your message on both sides:

> We buy houses
> 123-456-7891

Keep the message short: remember, drivers will have 5-7 seconds to get your number if they are driving by, and only a little longer if they are stopped at a red light.

Generating Buyer Leads

Contrary to what you probably heard elsewhere, I don't teach people to build their buyers' list first. One of the reasons I don't do this is that when I first got started I had this big MEGA list of buyers, probably 170 emails plus. I got my first deal together and NO ONE BOUGHT. The reason was I had a big list of tire kickers, wannabe's and some buyers who just did not want my deal.

As a wholesaler I don't target a specific area. It's always nice to get deals out of certain desirable areas, but just depending on that won't keep you in business long as a wholesaler. I go after the whole city. And sometimes you will get deals that a particular buyer does not want.

When you meet buyers ask them are they landlords, rehabbers or both. That way you know how to categorize them with your deals.

I went over a few ways to find buyers earlier but will go over them in detail here.

The first way to find buyers is to call "We buy houses" signs and Google "we buy houses (your city)". Call them up leave a message if need be, but the majority of the time they won't call back. That's normal: don't worry about that, because when sellers call them they often don't call them back either. If you have to leave a message it should go:

> HI my name is (your name)
> I am calling to see if you are a buyer or wholesaler.
> I will be having some deals coming up and would be curious to know
> if you are interested in buying them or partnering up with them on your
> list. If so please call me back at 123-456-7891

Once they call back, tell them that you are a wholesaler and you find deals and would be curious to know if they will buy them or be interested in partnering up to wholesale them. Also you are willing to split assignment fees on deals they bring a buyer in on.

If they are a buyer you get their information—name, phone number and email. You can ask them what are they looking for as well. Are they a landlord or buyer? Then put this information in Gmail (or whatever email system you use) under a contact folder named cash buyers.

If they are a wholesaler ask them if they are willing to partner up on deals and if you bring the sellers will they bring a buyer. If yes, then put this information in Gmail under a contact folder named cash buyers. Put in notes under their name that they are a wholesaler.

Town Foreclosure Auction

This is one of my best ways to pick up REAL cash buyers. Remember, the key to this is not to have this big gigantic list. You want real cash buyers who actually buy.

With this strategy you need to find out where your town does it local foreclosure auctions. And you must show up. You might want to have business cards to be taken a little bit more seriously. These guys have money, they don't like to waste time and are not big talkers because they think you are their competition. I sometimes have to tell them several times that I don't buy at the auction. I locate off-market properties that you do not have to get in bidding wars for.

Once they feel comfortable you should ask them for a card and make sure it has their number and email. The conversation should start like:

> Hello my name is NASAR.
> I am a wholesaler who finds off market properties at a DEEP discount. I was hoping to get your name, phone # and email for these properties.

Of course not everyone will be so accepting, but that's fine. Just move on and don't get stuck on the people who don't want your service.

Cash Transactions

Another way you can find REAL BUYERS is to look at the cash transactions in an area. This might require you to find a realtor who is okay with working with investors. Offer the realtor something, don't just take take take take—that is the quickest way to get your phone call sent to voice mail without getting a return call. Don't be that guy: offer the realtor your short sale leads, over priced leads and leads you just can't do anything with.

And don't expect anything in return right away. You will need this realtor to pull cash transactions more than just once, so you might want to bring something to the table. Also, not all realtors know they can do this. That is fine. Just work with realtors who are familiar with this. If you have a deal send them a flyer of your deal.

Another way you can get this list is buy it from Listsource.com or Flipthisrealestatelist.com

How to use listsource for market research and to get a buyers' list

1. Click "build list".
2. Choose your county or city.
3. Select for last market sale date a date six months in the past.
4. Under options, select absentee owners (in and out of state) and under corporate owned properties select no preference.

The resulting list will show you buyer activity to see if it is a viable city or county but will have properties purchased with a mortgage as well cash only activity. If you would like a cash only list go to flipthisrealestatelist.com.

Craig's List

Last, but not least, you can post ads on Craigslist.com saying you are looking for cash buyers who want to buy discount real estate. I do not advocate this and in my city you will get a bunch of unserious buyers who wouldn't buy even if you brought them the deal of the century. However your results may differ.

Summing Up

We are getting to near to the end, my friends. I went over the flipping houses process with no money or credit involved to buy the actual house. The process is simple but not easy. The most important thing you need to do with any entrepreneur endeavor is **change your mindset**.

I am not the same person I was when I first started. One of the main ingredients to my success was self-development. I jumped in it headfirst, because I knew to get me to a new, better place I had to pick some new, better habits. I stopped listening to music in the car and started listening to audiobooks, stopped watching TV and replaced that with reading, stopped partying and replaced that with Meetup groups focus around real estate. Don't be afraid of change.

The people around you now might not be the same people who will go with you to your destination. It's perfectly normal for people to place their own limitations onto others. Do not let those things get to you. If you are one of those people who are sensitive, do not tell anyone what you are trying to do. Just do it and, yes, it will be rough at first. However eventually it will get easier and better. People laughed at me and said I was stupid, that real estate doesn't work and I better focus on my job. I did not let those thing affect me.

Fast forward to now. This month alone I made $20k plus in assignment fees. Those naysayers are still at their jobs, sitting there hoping one day to hit the lottery while I'm creating my own future.

In conclusion, never forget the story of Jack Ma, a guy who could not get a job at KFC:

> Before I founded Alibaba, I invited 24 friends to my house to discuss the business opportunity. After discussing for a full two hours, they were still confused—I have to say that I may not have put myself across in a clear manner then. The verdict: 23 out of the 24 people in the room told me to drop the idea, for a multitude of reasons, such as: 'you do not know anything about the internet, and more prominently, you do not have the start-up capital for this' etc., etc.
>
> There was only one friend (who was working in a bank then) who told me, **"If you want to do it, just try it. If things don't work out the way you expect them to, you can always revert back to what you were doing before."** I pondered upon this for one night, and by the next morning, I decided I would do it anyway, even if all of the 24 people opposed the idea.

This guy is now the 70th richest man in the world. Never give up on your dreams.

Please be sure to subscribe to my YouTube channel. Youtube.com/realestatedoru and opt in to my blog at **realestatedoru.com**.

Thank for the support. I really mean that from the bottom of my heart. I wish you much success in your life and business.

About the Author

Nasar El-arabi worked several jobs after graduating from college, and quickly learned that the 9-5 corporate life was not for him. In 2012 Nasar lost his job, and had to decide whether to sink or swim. He decided to build a boat that would carry him over the roughest waters.

Since then Nasar has bought and sold over 100 homes, completing most of the deals using none of his own money or credit. Nasar has not only flipped houses like pancakes, he has inspired both youth and adults through his volunteer efforts in the community.

Made in the USA
Columbia, SC
11 February 2020

87786156R00022